Speak what you desire into existence

This manifestation journal belongs to

_____

Manifesting

_____

For more
inspirational content
follow us at:

ⓟ   @healforgiveletgo

◉   @healforgiveletgo

Join our email list:

✉   healforgiveletgo@gmail.com

PLEASE SUPPORT OUR SMALL BUSINESS BY LEAVING US A REVIEW ON AMAZON.

Manifest Your Dream Life

Although the author and publisher have made every effort to ensure that the information in this book was correct at press time, the author and publisher do not assume and hereby disclaim any liability to any party for any loss, damaged, or disruption caused by errors or omissions result from negligence, accident or any other cause.

This book is not intended as a substitute for the medical advice of a therapist. The reader should consult a therapist in matters relating to his/her/them health.

Manifestation

Manifestation - Using the power of your own mind to build your ideal life through intention setting and the belief that you already have what you want

Law of attraction - A belief that positive or negative thoughts bring positive or negative experiences into a person's life

Techniques

Vision board - Keep your dream life in front of your thoughts by looking at your vision board every day

Affirmation - One sentence statement to train your thoughts and beliefs towards a specific intention, repeat them to yourself or write them down every day

Gratitude - Simply write down what you are grateful for each day and inspire confidence in our ability to manifest even more positive things in the future

Manifestation Codes

Today I am manifesting this code........

Manifestation codes are numbers that you can repeat as affirmations or write down to activate. You can charge your crystal with intentions and send the codes as instructions.

For eg: I .... (your name) am going to activate the code - *** *** *** *** (insert number) for cash flow abundance on today .... (today's date)

Write your affirmations

_____
_____
_____
_____
_____
_____
_____
_____
_____
_____
_____
_____

Affirmations

I acknowledge my self-worth

Everything that is happening is for my own good

I am a powerhouse and indestructible

I am courageous and I stand up for my own self

I am filled with positivity and my life is prosperous

I will abandon my old habits and take up more positive ones today

Changing my mind is a strength

I affirm and encourage others and myself

I hold the truth of who I am

I am allowed to feel my best

I am capable of balancing ease and effort

I am complete as I am

Daily Ritual

Morning Rituals ☀️

_____
_____
_____
_____

Duration

_____
_____
_____
_____

Midday Rituals ☁️

_____
_____
_____
_____

Duration

_____
_____
_____
_____

Evening Rituals 🌙

_____
_____
_____
_____

Duration

_____
_____
_____
_____

Notes

_____
_____
_____
_____

3-6-9 Method

For the 369 manifestation technique, you'll write down your manifestation every day, 3 times in the morning, 6 times in the afternoon, and 9 times at night.

Morning Affirmations

_____

_____

_____

Midday Affirmations

_____

_____

_____

_____

_____

_____

Evening Affirmations

_____

_____

_____

_____

_____

_____

_____

_____

_____

Your Desires

Defining my desires

Stating my reasons

How would I feel

Gratitude

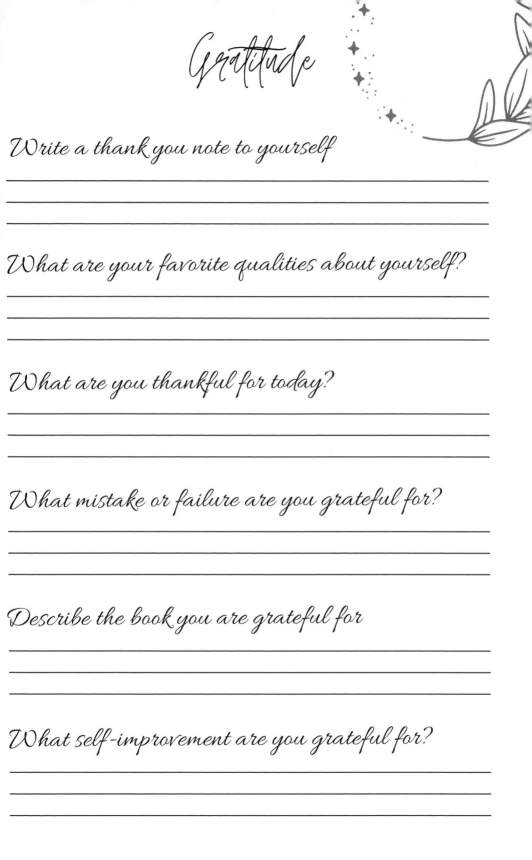

Write a thank you note to yourself

_____
_____
_____

What are your favorite qualities about yourself?

_____
_____
_____

What are you thankful for today?

_____
_____
_____

What mistake or failure are you grateful for?

_____
_____
_____

Describe the book you are grateful for

_____
_____
_____

What self-improvement are you grateful for?

_____
_____
_____

Dream Board
Vision & Aspirations

Career

_____
_____
_____
_____
_____

Health

_____
_____
_____
_____

Hobbies

_____
_____
_____
_____

Travel

_____
_____
_____
_____

Relationships

_____
_____
_____
_____

Manifest

What I want to manifest?

_____
_____
_____
_____
_____
_____
_____
_____

Why I want to manifest it?

_____
_____
_____
_____
_____
_____
_____

How will I manifest it?

_____
_____
_____
_____
_____
_____
_____
_____

Small steps to manifest it.

Scripting

How to script your manifestations into existence

- Be very clear and specific about what you desire
- Use one of the scribble pages to write down your manifestation. Use present or past tense, to show that you have already manifested it
- Feel the same emotions as if you already had it. You can accomplish this by imagining the sounds, the smell, the actual visuals of how it'd feel to touch or hold the thing you are manifesting.
- Finish it off by expressing a ton of gratitude to the universe for delivering your blessing in a divinely timed manner.
- Close your journal and know that it is done. Don't worry about when or how you'll receive the blessing, just know that you have scripted it, it is yours and you will soon see it in physical form.

Scribble

Manifestation Prompts

I can make my life easier by
I am achieving this goal because
My future self is . . . .
I express love to my partner by
I feel comforted and loved when
I am lovable because
This is what I am willing to receive
I am willing to release
I am embracing a wealthy lifestyle by
My mindset is changing by
I deserve abundance because
I see abundance in
I am attracting miracles by
I affirm that the love I want is
What am I currently appreciating?
I am loving...
Past moments that were so beautiful...
Things I love about this life journey...
In my dream, who do I see?

Scribble

Answer your favorite prompts here

_____
_____
_____
_____
_____
_____
_____
_____
_____
_____
_____
_____
_____
_____
_____
_____
_____
_____
_____
_____
_____
_____
_____
_____
_____
_____
_____
_____
_____
_____
_____
_____
_____
_____

Manifestation Codes

Today I am manifesting this code........

Manifestation codes are numbers that you can repeat as affirmations or write down to activate. You can charge your crystal with intentions and send the codes as instructions.

For eg: I .... (your name) am going to activate the code - *** *** *** *** (insert number) for cash flow abundance on today .... (today's date)

Write your affirmations

_____
_____
_____
_____
_____
_____
_____
_____
_____
_____
_____
_____

Affirmations

I acknowledge my self-worth
Everything that is happening is for my own
good
I am a powerhouse and indestructible
I am courageous and I stand up for my own self
I am filled with positivity and my life is
prosperous

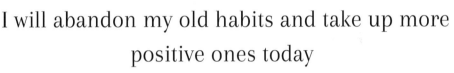

I will abandon my old habits and take up more
positive ones today
Changing my mind is a strength
I affirm and encourage others and myself
I hold the truth of who I am
I am allowed to feel my best
I am capable of balancing ease and effort
I am complete as I am

Daily Ritual

Morning Rituals ☀

Duration

_____
_____
_____
_____

_____
_____
_____
_____

Midday Rituals ☁

Duration

_____
_____
_____
_____

_____
_____
_____
_____

Evening Rituals 🌙

Duration

_____
_____
_____
_____

_____
_____
_____
_____

Notes

_____
_____
_____
_____
_____

3-6-9 Method

For the 369 manifestation technique, you'll write down your manifestation every day, 3 times in the morning, 6 times in the afternoon, and 9 times at night.

Morning Affirmations

_____
_____
_____

Midday Affirmations

_____
_____
_____
_____
_____
_____

Evening Affirmations

_____
_____
_____
_____
_____
_____
_____
_____
_____

Your Desires

Defining my desires

Stating my reasons

How would I feel

Gratitude

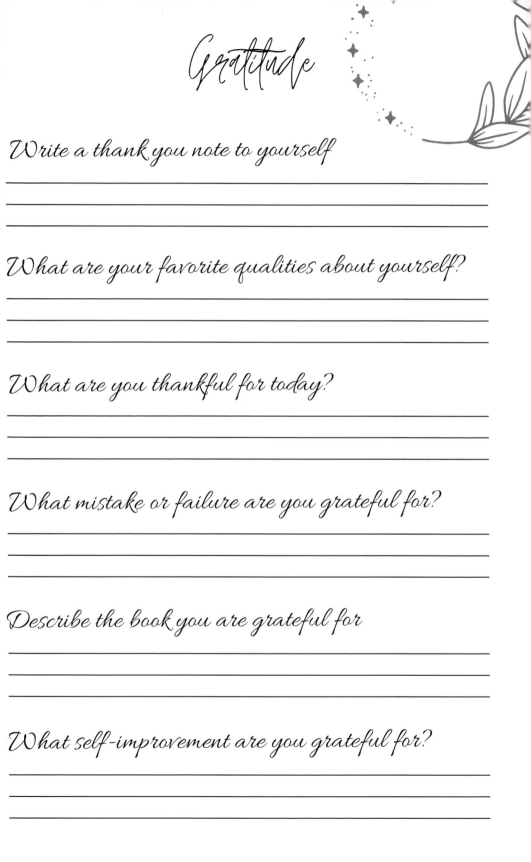

Write a thank you note to yourself

_____
_____
_____

What are your favorite qualities about yourself?

_____
_____
_____

What are you thankful for today?

_____
_____
_____

What mistake or failure are you grateful for?

_____
_____
_____

Describe the book you are grateful for

_____
_____
_____

What self-improvement are you grateful for?

_____
_____
_____

Dream Board
Vision & Aspirations

Career
_____
_____
_____
_____
_____

Health
_____
_____
_____
_____
_____

Hobbies
_____
_____
_____
_____
_____

Travel
_____
_____
_____
_____
_____

Relationships
_____
_____
_____
_____
_____

Manifest

What I want to manifest?

_____
_____
_____
_____
_____
_____
_____
_____

Why I want to manifest it?

_____
_____
_____
_____
_____
_____
_____

How will I manifest it?

_____
_____
_____
_____
_____
_____
_____
_____

Small steps to manifest it.

Scripting

How to script your manifestations into existence

- Be very clear and specific about what you desire

- Use one of the scribble pages to write down your manifestation. Use present or past tense, to show that you have already manifested it

- Feel the same emotions as if you already had it. You can accomplish this by imagining the sounds, the smell, the actual visuals of how it'd feel to touch or hold the thing you are manifesting.

- Finish it off by expressing a ton of gratitude to the universe for delivering your blessing in a divinely timed manner.

- Close your journal and know that it is done. Don't worry about when or how you'll receive the blessing, just know that you have scripted it, it is yours and you will soon see it in physical form.

Scribble

Manifestation Prompts

I can make my life easier by

I am achieving this goal because

My future self is . . . .

I express love to my partner by

I feel comforted and loved when

I am lovable because

This is what I am willing to receive

I am willing to release

I am embracing a wealthy lifestyle by

My mindset is changing by

I deserve abundance because

I see abundance in

I am attracting miracles by

I affirm that the love I want is

What am I currently appreciating?

I am loving...

Past moments that were so beautiful...

Things I love about this life journey...

In my dream, who do I see?

Scribble

Answer your favorite prompts here

_____
_____
_____
_____
_____
_____
_____
_____
_____
_____
_____
_____
_____
_____
_____
_____
_____
_____
_____
_____
_____
_____
_____
_____
_____
_____
_____
_____
_____
_____
_____
_____

Manifestation Codes

Today I am manifesting this code........

Manifestation codes are numbers that you can repeat as affirmations or write down to activate. You can charge your crystal with intentions and send the codes as instructions.

For eg: I .... (your name) am going to activate the code - *** *** *** *** (insert number) for cash flow abundance on today .... (today's date)

Write your affirmations

_____
_____
_____
_____
_____
_____
_____
_____
_____
_____
_____
_____

Affirmations

I acknowledge my self-worth
Everything that is happening is for my own
good
I am a powerhouse and indestructible
I am courageous and I stand up for my own self
I am filled with positivity and my life is
prosperous
I will abandon my old habits and take up more
positive ones today
Changing my mind is a strength
I affirm and encourage others and myself
I hold the truth of who I am
I am allowed to feel my best
I am capable of balancing ease and effort
I am complete as I am

Daily Ritual

Morning Rituals ☀

Duration

_____
_____
_____
_____

Midday Rituals ☁

Duration

_____
_____
_____
_____

Evening Rituals 🌙

Duration

_____
_____
_____
_____

Notes

_____
_____
_____
_____

3-6-9 Method

For the 369 manifestation technique, you'll write down your manifestation every day, 3 times in the morning, 6 times in the afternoon, and 9 times at night.

Morning Affirmations

_____
_____
_____

Midday Affirmations

_____
_____
_____
_____
_____
_____

Evening Affirmations

_____
_____
_____
_____
_____
_____
_____
_____
_____

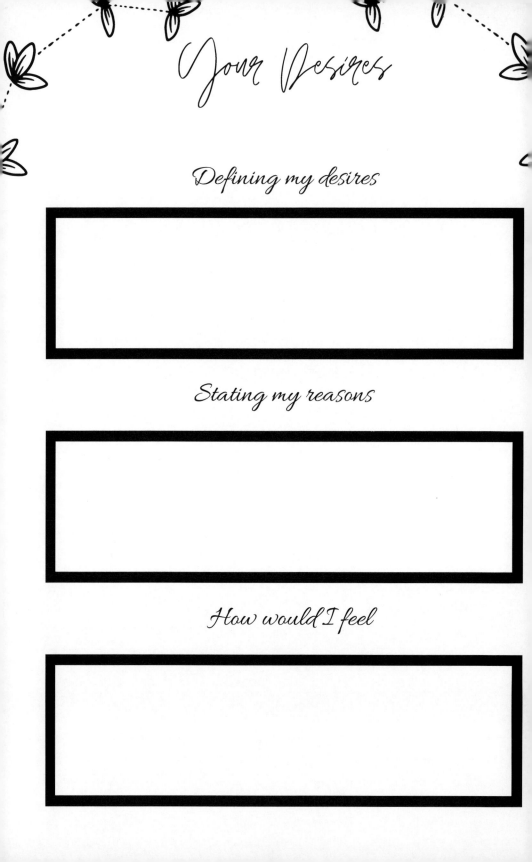

Your Desires

Defining my desires

Stating my reasons

How would I feel

Gratitude

Write a thank you note to yourself

_____
_____
_____

What are your favorite qualities about yourself?

_____
_____
_____

What are you thankful for today?

_____
_____
_____

What mistake or failure are you grateful for?

_____
_____
_____

Describe the book you are grateful for

_____
_____
_____

What self-improvement are you grateful for?

_____
_____
_____

Dream Board

Vision & Aspirations

Career

_____
_____
_____
_____

Health

_____
_____
_____
_____

Hobbies

_____
_____
_____
_____

Travel

_____
_____
_____
_____

Relationships

_____
_____
_____
_____

Manifest

What I want to manifest?

_____
_____
_____
_____
_____
_____
_____
_____

Why I want to manifest it?

_____
_____
_____
_____
_____
_____
_____

How will I manifest it?

_____
_____
_____
_____
_____
_____
_____
_____
_____
_____

Small steps to manifest it.

Scripting

How to script your manifestations into existence

- Be very clear and specific about what you desire
- Use one of the scribble pages to write down your manifestation. Use present or past tense, to show that you have already manifested it
- Feel the same emotions as if you already had it. You can accomplish this by imagining the sounds, the smell, the actual visuals of how it'd feel to touch or hold the thing you are manifesting.
- Finish it off by expressing a ton of gratitude to the universe for delivering your blessing in a divinely timed manner.
- Close your journal and know that it is done. Don't worry about when or how you'll receive the blessing, just know that you have scripted it, it is yours and you will soon see it in physical form.

Scribble

Manifestation Prompts

I can make my life easier by
I am achieving this goal because
My future self is . . . .
I express love to my partner by
I feel comforted and loved when
I am lovable because
This is what I am willing to receive
I am willing to release
I am embracing a wealthy lifestyle by
My mindset is changing by
I deserve abundance because
I see abundance in
I am attracting miracles by
I affirm that the love I want is
What am I currently appreciating?
I am loving...
Past moments that were so beautiful...
Things I love about this life journey...
In my dream, who do I see?

Scribble

Answer your favorite prompts here

Manifestation Codes

Today I am manifesting this code........

Manifestation codes are numbers that you can repeat as affirmations or write down to activate. You can charge your crystal with intentions and send the codes as instructions.

For eg: I .... (your name) am going to activate the code - *** *** *** *** (insert number) for cash flow abundance on today .... (today's date)

Write your affirmations

_____
_____
_____
_____
_____
_____
_____
_____
_____
_____
_____
_____
_____
_____

Affirmations

I acknowledge my self-worth

Everything that is happening is for my own good

I am a powerhouse and indestructible

I am courageous and I stand up for my own self

I am filled with positivity and my life is prosperous

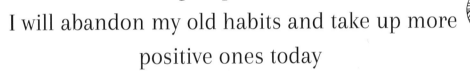

I will abandon my old habits and take up more positive ones today

Changing my mind is a strength

I affirm and encourage others and myself

I hold the truth of who I am

I am allowed to feel my best

I am capable of balancing ease and effort

I am complete as I am

Daily Ritual

Morning Rituals ☀️

_____
_____
_____
_____

Duration

_____
_____
_____
_____

Midday Rituals ☁️

_____
_____
_____
_____

Duration

_____
_____
_____
_____

Evening Rituals 🌙

_____
_____
_____
_____

Duration

_____
_____
_____
_____

Notes

_____
_____
_____
_____
_____

3-6-9 Method

For the 369 manifestation technique, you'll write down your manifestation every day, 3 times in the morning, 6 times in the afternoon, and 9 times at night.

Morning Affirmations

_____
_____
_____

Midday Affirmations

_____
_____
_____
_____
_____
_____

Evening Affirmations

_____
_____
_____
_____
_____
_____
_____
_____
_____

Your Desires

Defining my desires

Stating my reasons

How would I feel

Gratitude

Write a thank you note to yourself
_____
_____
_____

What are your favorite qualities about yourself?
_____
_____
_____

What are you thankful for today?
_____
_____
_____

What mistake or failure are you grateful for?
_____
_____
_____

Describe the book you are grateful for
_____
_____
_____

What self-improvement are you grateful for?
_____
_____
_____

Dream Board

Vision & Aspirations

Career

_____
_____
_____
_____

Health

_____
_____
_____
_____

Hobbies

_____
_____
_____
_____

Travel

_____
_____
_____
_____

Relationships

_____
_____
_____
_____

Manifest

What I want to manifest?

_____
_____
_____
_____
_____
_____
_____
_____

Why I want to manifest it?

_____
_____
_____
_____
_____
_____
_____

How will I manifest it?

_____
_____
_____
_____
_____
_____
_____
_____
_____

Small steps to manifest it.

Scripting

How to script your manifestations into existence

- Be very clear and specific about what you desire
- Use one of the scribble pages to write down your manifestation. Use present or past tense, to show that you have already manifested it
- Feel the same emotions as if you already had it. You can accomplish this by imagining the sounds, the smell, the actual visuals of how it'd feel to touch or hold the thing you are manifesting.
- Finish it off by expressing a ton of gratitude to the universe for delivering your blessing in a divinely timed manner.
- Close your journal and know that it is done. Don't worry about when or how you'll receive the blessing, just know that you have scripted it, it is yours and you will soon see it in physical form.

Scribble

Manifestation Prompts

I can make my life easier by

I am achieving this goal because

My future self is . . . .

I express love to my partner by

I feel comforted and loved when

I am lovable because

This is what I am willing to receive

I am willing to release

I am embracing a wealthy lifestyle by

My mindset is changing by

I deserve abundance because

I see abundance in

I am attracting miracles by

I affirm that the love I want is

What am I currently appreciating?

I am loving...

Past moments that were so beautiful...

Things I love about this life journey...

In my dream, who do I see?

Scribble

Answer your favorite prompts here

Manifestation Codes

Today I am manifesting this code........

Manifestation codes are numbers that you can repeat as affirmations or write down to activate. You can charge your crystal with intentions and send the codes as instructions.

For eg: I .... (your name) am going to activate the code - *** *** *** *** (insert number) for cash flow abundance on today .... (today's date)

Write your affirmations

_____
_____
_____
_____
_____
_____
_____
_____
_____
_____
_____
_____

Affirmations

I acknowledge my self-worth

Everything that is happening is for my own good

I am a powerhouse and indestructible

I am courageous and I stand up for my own self

I am filled with positivity and my life is prosperous

I will abandon my old habits and take up more positive ones today

Changing my mind is a strength

I affirm and encourage others and myself

I hold the truth of who I am

I am allowed to feel my best

I am capable of balancing ease and effort

I am complete as I am

Daily Ritual

Morning Rituals ☀

Duration

Midday Rituals ☁

Duration

Evening Rituals 🌙

Duration

Notes

3-6-9 Method

For the 369 manifestation technique, you'll write down your manifestation every day, 3 times in the morning, 6 times in the afternoon, and 9 times at night.

Morning Affirmations

_____
_____
_____

Midday Affirmations

_____
_____
_____
_____
_____
_____

Evening Affirmations

_____
_____
_____
_____
_____
_____
_____
_____
_____

Your Desires

Defining my desires

Stating my reasons

How would I feel

Gratitude

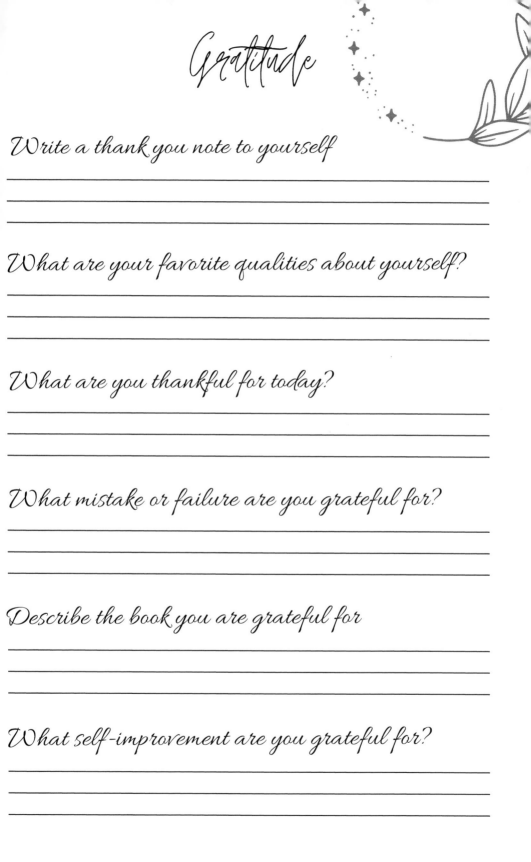

Write a thank you note to yourself

_____
_____
_____

What are your favorite qualities about yourself?

_____
_____
_____

What are you thankful for today?

_____
_____
_____

What mistake or failure are you grateful for?

_____
_____
_____

Describe the book you are grateful for

_____
_____
_____

What self-improvement are you grateful for?

_____
_____
_____

Dream Board

Vision & Aspirations

Career

_____
_____
_____
_____
_____

Health

_____
_____
_____
_____
_____

Hobbies

_____
_____
_____
_____
_____

Travel

_____
_____
_____
_____
_____

Relationships

_____
_____
_____
_____
_____

Manifest

What I want to manifest?

_____
_____
_____
_____
_____
_____
_____
_____

Why I want to manifest it?

_____
_____
_____
_____
_____
_____
_____
_____

How will I manifest it?

_____
_____
_____
_____
_____
_____
_____
_____

Small steps to manifest it.

Scripting

How to script your manifestations into existence

- Be very clear and specific about what you desire
- Use one of the scribble pages to write down your manifestation. Use present or past tense, to show that you have already manifested it
- Feel the same emotions as if you already had it. You can accomplish this by imagining the sounds, the smell, the actual visuals of how it'd feel to touch or hold the thing you are manifesting.
- Finish it off by expressing a ton of gratitude to the universe for delivering your blessing in a divinely timed manner.
- Close your journal and know that it is done. Don't worry about when or how you'll receive the blessing, just know that you have scripted it, it is yours and you will soon see it in physical form.

Scribble

Manifestation Prompts

I can make my life easier by

I am achieving this goal because

My future self is . . . .

I express love to my partner by

I feel comforted and loved when

I am lovable because

This is what I am willing to receive

I am willing to release

I am embracing a wealthy lifestyle by

My mindset is changing by

I deserve abundance because

I see abundance in

I am attracting miracles by

I affirm that the love I want is

What am I currently appreciating?

I am loving...

Past moments that were so beautiful...

Things I love about this life journey...

In my dream, who do I see?

Scribble

Answer your favorite prompts here

Manifestation Codes

Today I am manifesting this code........

Manifestation codes are numbers that you can repeat as affirmations or write down to activate. You can charge your crystal with intentions and send the codes as instructions.

For eg: I .... (your name) am going to activate the code - *** *** *** *** (insert number) for cash flow abundance on today .... (today's date)

Write your affirmations

_____

_____

_____

_____

_____

_____

_____

_____

_____

_____

_____

_____

_____

_____

Affirmations

I acknowledge my self-worth

Everything that is happening is for my own good

I am a powerhouse and indestructible

I am courageous and I stand up for my own self

I am filled with positivity and my life is prosperous

I will abandon my old habits and take up more positive ones today

Changing my mind is a strength

I affirm and encourage others and myself

I hold the truth of who I am

I am allowed to feel my best

I am capable of balancing ease and effort

I am complete as I am

Daily Ritual

Morning Rituals ☀

Duration

_____
_____
_____
_____

Midday Rituals ☁

Duration

_____
_____
_____
_____

Evening Rituals 🌙

Duration

_____
_____
_____
_____

Notes

_____
_____
_____
_____
_____

3-6-9 Method

For the 369 manifestation technique, you'll write down your manifestation every day, 3 times in the morning, 6 times in the afternoon, and 9 times at night.

Morning Affirmations

_____
_____
_____

Midday Affirmations

_____
_____
_____
_____
_____
_____

Evening Affirmations

_____
_____
_____
_____
_____
_____
_____
_____
_____

Your Desires

Defining my desires

Stating my reasons

How would I feel

Gratitude

Write a thank you note to yourself

_____
_____
_____

What are your favorite qualities about yourself?

_____
_____
_____

What are you thankful for today?

_____
_____
_____

What mistake or failure are you grateful for?

_____
_____
_____

Describe the book you are grateful for

_____
_____
_____

What self-improvement are you grateful for?

_____
_____
_____

Dream Board
Vision & Aspirations

Career
_____
_____
_____
_____

Health
_____
_____
_____
_____

Hobbies
_____
_____
_____
_____

Travel
_____
_____
_____
_____

Relationships
_____
_____
_____
_____

Manifest

What I want to manifest?

_____
_____
_____
_____
_____
_____
_____

Why I want to manifest it?

_____
_____
_____
_____
_____
_____
_____

How will I manifest it?

_____
_____
_____
_____
_____
_____
_____
_____
_____

Small steps to manifest it.

Scripting

How to script your manifestations into existence

- Be very clear and specific about what you desire
- Use one of the scribble pages to write down your manifestation. Use present or past tense, to show that you have already manifested it
- Feel the same emotions as if you already had it. You can accomplish this by imagining the sounds, the smell, the actual visuals of how it'd feel to touch or hold the thing you are manifesting.
- Finish it off by expressing a ton of gratitude to the universe for delivering your blessing in a divinely timed manner.
- Close your journal and know that it is done. Don't worry about when or how you'll receive the blessing, just know that you have scripted it, it is yours and you will soon see it in physical form.

Scribble

Manifestation Prompts

I can make my life easier by
I am achieving this goal because
My future self is . . . .
I express love to my partner by
I feel comforted and loved when
I am lovable because
This is what I am willing to receive
I am willing to release
I am embracing a wealthy lifestyle by
My mindset is changing by
I deserve abundance because
I see abundance in
I am attracting miracles by
I affirm that the love I want is
What am I currently appreciating?
I am loving...
Past moments that were so beautiful...
Things I love about this life journey...
In my dream, who do I see?

Scribble

Answer your favorite prompts here

_____
_____
_____
_____
_____
_____
_____
_____
_____
_____
_____
_____
_____
_____
_____
_____
_____
_____
_____
_____
_____
_____
_____
_____
_____
_____
_____
_____
_____
_____
_____

Manifestation Codes

Today I am manifesting this code........

Manifestation codes are numbers that you can repeat as affirmations or write down to activate. You can charge your crystal with intentions and send the codes as instructions.

For eg: I .... (your name) am going to activate the code - *** *** *** *** (insert number) for cash flow abundance on today .... (today's date)

Write your affirmations

_____
_____
_____
_____
_____
_____
_____
_____
_____
_____
_____
_____
_____
_____

Affirmations

I acknowledge my self-worth

Everything that is happening is for my own good

I am a powerhouse and indestructible

I am courageous and I stand up for my own self

I am filled with positivity and my life is prosperous

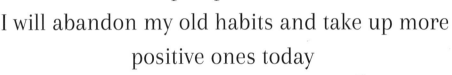

I will abandon my old habits and take up more positive ones today

Changing my mind is a strength

I affirm and encourage others and myself

I hold the truth of who I am

I am allowed to feel my best

I am capable of balancing ease and effort

I am complete as I am

Daily Ritual

Morning Rituals ☀

Duration

_____
_____
_____
_____

Midday Rituals ☁

Duration

_____
_____
_____
_____

Evening Rituals ☾

Duration

_____
_____
_____
_____

Notes

_____
_____
_____
_____
_____

3-6-9 Method

For the 369 manifestation technique, you'll write down your manifestation every day, 3 times in the morning, 6 times in the afternoon, and 9 times at night.

Morning Affirmations

_____

_____

_____

Midday Affirmations

_____

_____

_____

_____

_____

_____

Evening Affirmations

_____

_____

_____

_____

_____

_____

_____

_____

_____

Your Desires

Defining my desires

Stating my reasons

How would I feel

Gratitude

Write a thank you note to yourself
_____
_____
_____

What are your favorite qualities about yourself?
_____
_____
_____

What are you thankful for today?
_____
_____
_____

What mistake or failure are you grateful for?
_____
_____
_____

Describe the book you are grateful for
_____
_____
_____

What self-improvement are you grateful for?
_____
_____
_____

Dream Board
Vision & Aspirations

Career

_____
_____
_____
_____
_____

Health

_____
_____
_____
_____
_____

Hobbies

_____
_____
_____
_____
_____

Travel

_____
_____
_____
_____
_____

Relationships

_____
_____
_____
_____
_____

Manifest

What I want to manifest?

_____
_____
_____
_____
_____
_____
_____
_____

Why I want to manifest it?

_____
_____
_____
_____
_____
_____
_____
_____

How will I manifest it?

_____
_____
_____
_____
_____
_____
_____
_____
_____
_____

Small steps to manifest it.

Scripting

How to script your manifestations into existence

- Be very clear and specific about what you desire
- Use one of the scribble pages to write down your manifestation. Use present or past tense, to show that you have already manifested it
- Feel the same emotions as if you already had it. You can accomplish this by imagining the sounds, the smell, the actual visuals of how it'd feel to touch or hold the thing you are manifesting.
- Finish it off by expressing a ton of gratitude to the universe for delivering your blessing in a divinely timed manner.
- Close your journal and know that it is done. Don't worry about when or how you'll receive the blessing, just know that you have scripted it, it is yours and you will soon see it in physical form.

Scribble

Manifestation Prompts

I can make my life easier by

I am achieving this goal because

My future self is . . . .

I express love to my partner by

I feel comforted and loved when

I am lovable because

This is what I am willing to receive

I am willing to release

I am embracing a wealthy lifestyle by

My mindset is changing by

I deserve abundance because

I see abundance in

I am attracting miracles by

I affirm that the love I want is

What am I currently appreciating?

I am loving...

Past moments that were so beautiful...

Things I love about this life journey...

In my dream, who do I see?

Scribble

Answer your favorite prompts here

Manifestation Codes

Today I am manifesting this code........

Manifestation codes are numbers that you can repeat as affirmations or write down to activate. You can charge your crystal with intentions and send the codes as instructions.

For eg: I .... (your name) am going to activate the code - *** *** *** *** (insert number) for cash flow abundance on today .... (today's date)

Write your affirmations

_____
_____
_____
_____
_____
_____
_____
_____
_____
_____
_____
_____

Affirmations

I acknowledge my self-worth

Everything that is happening is for my own good

I am a powerhouse and indestructible

I am courageous and I stand up for my own self

I am filled with positivity and my life is prosperous

I will abandon my old habits and take up more positive ones today

Changing my mind is a strength

I affirm and encourage others and myself

I hold the truth of who I am

I am allowed to feel my best

I am capable of balancing ease and effort

I am complete as I am

Daily Ritual

Morning Rituals ☀

Duration

_____
_____
_____
_____

Midday Rituals ☁

Duration

_____
_____
_____
_____

Evening Rituals 🌙

Duration

_____
_____
_____
_____

Notes

_____
_____
_____
_____

3-6-9 Method

For the 369 manifestation technique, you'll write down your manifestation every day, 3 times in the morning, 6 times in the afternoon, and 9 times at night.

Morning Affirmations

_____

_____

_____

Midday Affirmations

_____

_____

_____

_____

_____

_____

Evening Affirmations

_____

_____

_____

_____

_____

_____

_____

_____

_____

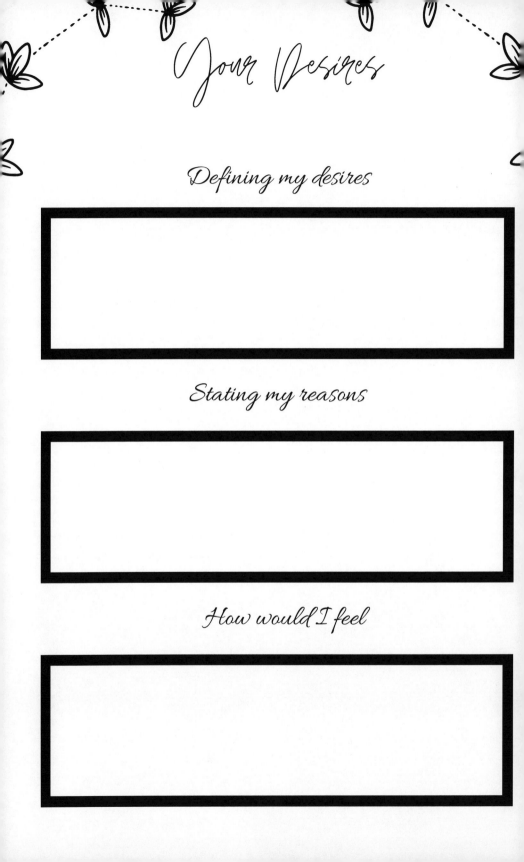

Your Desires

Defining my desires

Stating my reasons

How would I feel

Gratitude

Write a thank you note to yourself

_____
_____
_____

What are your favorite qualities about yourself?

_____
_____
_____

What are you thankful for today?

_____
_____
_____

What mistake or failure are you grateful for?

_____
_____
_____

Describe the book you are grateful for

_____
_____
_____

What self-improvement are you grateful for?

_____
_____
_____

Dream Board
Vision & Aspirations

Career
_____
_____
_____
_____

Health
_____
_____
_____
_____

Hobbies
_____
_____
_____
_____

Travel
_____
_____
_____
_____

Relationships
_____
_____
_____
_____

Manifest

What I want to manifest?

_____
_____
_____
_____
_____
_____
_____
_____

Why I want to manifest it?

_____
_____
_____
_____
_____
_____
_____
_____

How will I manifest it?

_____
_____
_____
_____
_____
_____
_____
_____
_____

Small steps to manifest it.

Scripting

How to script your manifestations into existence

- Be very clear and specific about what you desire
- Use one of the scribble pages to write down your manifestation. Use present or past tense, to show that you have already manifested it
- Feel the same emotions as if you already had it. You can accomplish this by imagining the sounds, the smell, the actual visuals of how it'd feel to touch or hold the thing you are manifesting.
- Finish it off by expressing a ton of gratitude to the universe for delivering your blessing in a divinely timed manner.
- Close your journal and know that it is done. Don't worry about when or how you'll receive the blessing, just know that you have scripted it, it is yours and you will soon see it in physical form.

Scribble

Manifestation Prompts

I can make my life easier by

I am achieving this goal because

My future self is . . . .

I express love to my partner by

I feel comforted and loved when

I am lovable because

This is what I am willing to receive

I am willing to release

 I am embracing a wealthy lifestyle by

My mindset is changing by

I deserve abundance because

I see abundance in

I am attracting miracles by

I affirm that the love I want is

What am I currently appreciating?

I am loving...

Past moments that were so beautiful...

Things I love about this life journey...

In my dream, who do I see?

Scribble

Answer your favorite prompts here

Manifestation Codes

Today I am manifesting this code........

Manifestation codes are numbers that you can repeat as affirmations or write down to activate. You can charge your crystal with intentions and send the codes as instructions.

For eg: I .... (your name) am going to activate the code - *** *** *** *** (insert number) for cash flow abundance on today .... (today's date)

Write your affirmations

_____
_____
_____
_____
_____
_____
_____
_____
_____
_____
_____
_____

Affirmations

I acknowledge my self-worth
Everything that is happening is for my own
good
I am a powerhouse and indestructible
I am courageous and I stand up for my own self
I am filled with positivity and my life is
prosperous
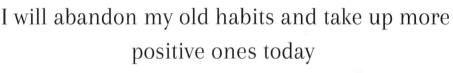
I will abandon my old habits and take up more
positive ones today
Changing my mind is a strength
I affirm and encourage others and myself
I hold the truth of who I am
I am allowed to feel my best
I am capable of balancing ease and effort
I am complete as I am

Daily Ritual

Morning Rituals ☀

Duration

_____
_____
_____
_____

Midday Rituals ☁

Duration

_____
_____
_____
_____

Evening Rituals 🌙

Duration

_____
_____
_____
_____

Notes

_____
_____
_____
_____
_____

3-6-9 Method

For the 369 manifestation technique, you'll write down your manifestation every day, 3 times in the morning, 6 times in the afternoon, and 9 times at night.

Morning Affirmations

_____
_____
_____

Midday Affirmations

_____
_____
_____
_____
_____
_____

Evening Affirmations

_____
_____
_____
_____
_____
_____
_____
_____
_____

Your Desires

Defining my desires

Stating my reasons

How would I feel

Gratitude

Write a thank you note to yourself

_____
_____
_____

What are your favorite qualities about yourself?

_____
_____
_____

What are you thankful for today?

_____
_____
_____

What mistake or failure are you grateful for?

_____
_____
_____

Describe the book you are grateful for

_____
_____
_____

What self-improvement are you grateful for?

_____
_____
_____

Dream Board
Vision & Aspirations

Career
_____
_____
_____
_____
_____

Health
_____
_____
_____
_____
_____

Hobbies
_____
_____
_____
_____
_____

Travel
_____
_____
_____
_____
_____

Relationships
_____
_____
_____
_____
_____

Manifest

What I want to manifest?

_____
_____
_____
_____
_____
_____
_____

Why I want to manifest it?

_____
_____
_____
_____
_____
_____
_____

How will I manifest it?

_____
_____
_____
_____
_____
_____
_____
_____
_____

Small steps to manifest it.

Scripting

How to script your manifestations into existence

- Be very clear and specific about what you desire
- Use one of the scribble pages to write down your manifestation. Use present or past tense, to show that you have already manifested it
- Feel the same emotions as if you already had it. You can accomplish this by imagining the sounds, the smell, the actual visuals of how it'd feel to touch or hold the thing you are manifesting.
- Finish it off by expressing a ton of gratitude to the universe for delivering your blessing in a divinely timed manner.
- Close your journal and know that it is done. Don't worry about when or how you'll receive the blessing, just know that you have scripted it, it is yours and you will soon see it in physical form.

Scribble

Manifestation Prompts

I can make my life easier by

I am achieving this goal because

My future self is . . . .

I express love to my partner by

I feel comforted and loved when

I am lovable because

This is what I am willing to receive

I am willing to release

I am embracing a wealthy lifestyle by

My mindset is changing by

I deserve abundance because

I see abundance in

I am attracting miracles by

I affirm that the love I want is

What am I currently appreciating?

I am loving...

Past moments that were so beautiful...

Things I love about this life journey...

In my dream, who do I see?

Scribble

Answer your favorite prompts here

Manifestation Codes

Today I am manifesting this code........

Manifestation codes are numbers that you can repeat as affirmations or write down to activate. You can charge your crystal with intentions and send the codes as instructions.

For eg: I .... (your name) am going to activate the code - *** *** *** *** (insert number) for cash flow abundance on today .... (today's date)

Write your affirmations

_____
_____
_____
_____
_____
_____
_____
_____
_____
_____
_____
_____

Affirmations

I acknowledge my self-worth

Everything that is happening is for my own good

I am a powerhouse and indestructible

I am courageous and I stand up for my own self

I am filled with positivity and my life is prosperous

I will abandon my old habits and take up more positive ones today

Changing my mind is a strength

I affirm and encourage others and myself

I hold the truth of who I am

I am allowed to feel my best

I am capable of balancing ease and effort

I am complete as I am

Daily Ritual

Morning Rituals ☀

Duration

_____
_____
_____
_____

Midday Rituals ☁

Duration

_____
_____
_____
_____

Evening Rituals 🌙

Duration

_____
_____
_____
_____

Notes

_____
_____
_____
_____
_____

3-6-9 Method

For the 369 manifestation technique, you'll write down your manifestation every day, 3 times in the morning, 6 times in the afternoon, and 9 times at night.

Morning Affirmations

_____
_____
_____

Midday Affirmations

_____
_____
_____
_____
_____
_____

Evening Affirmations

_____
_____
_____
_____
_____
_____
_____
_____
_____

Your Desires

Defining my desires

Stating my reasons

How would I feel

Gratitude

Write a thank you note to yourself

_____
_____
_____

What are your favorite qualities about yourself?

_____
_____
_____

What are you thankful for today?

_____
_____
_____

What mistake or failure are you grateful for?

_____
_____
_____

Describe the book you are grateful for

_____
_____
_____

What self-improvement are you grateful for?

_____
_____
_____

Dream Board
Vision & Aspirations

Career

_____
_____
_____
_____
_____

Health

_____
_____
_____
_____
_____

Hobbies

_____
_____
_____
_____
_____

Travel

_____
_____
_____
_____
_____

Relationships

_____
_____
_____
_____
_____

Scripting

How to script your manifestations into existence

- Be very clear and specific about what you desire
- Use one of the scribble pages to write down your manifestation. Use present or past tense, to show that you have already manifested it
- Feel the same emotions as if you already had it. You can accomplish this by imagining the sounds, the smell, the actual visuals of how it'd feel to touch or hold the thing you are manifesting.
- Finish it off by expressing a ton of gratitude to the universe for delivering your blessing in a divinely timed manner.
- Close your journal and know that it is done. Don't worry about when or how you'll receive the blessing, just know that you have scripted it, it is yours and you will soon see it in physical form.

Scribble

Scribble

Answer your favorite prompts here

_____
_____
_____
_____
_____
_____
_____
_____
_____
_____
_____
_____
_____
_____
_____
_____
_____
_____
_____
_____
_____
_____
_____
_____
_____
_____
_____
_____
_____
_____
_____
_____
_____